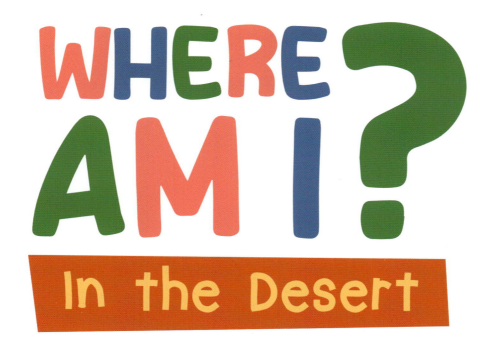

Written by Noah Leatherland

Published in 2025 by Enslow Publishing, LLC
2544 Clinton Street
Buffalo, NY 14224

© 2024 BookLife Publishing Ltd.

Written by:
Noah Leatherland

Edited by:
Rebecca Phillips-Bartlett

Designed by:
Amy Li

Cataloging-in-Publication Data

Names: Leatherland, Noah, 1999-.
Title: In the desert / Noah Leatherland.
Description: Buffalo, NY : Enslow Publishing, 2025. | Series: Where am I? | Includes glossary.
Identifiers: ISBN 9781978541719 (pbk.) | ISBN 9781978541726 (library bound) | ISBN 9781978541733 (ebook)
Subjects: LCSH: Desert animals--Habitation--Juvenile literature. | Desert animals--Juvenile literature.
Classification: LCC QL116.L38 2025 | DDC 591.754--dc23

All rights reserved.

No part of this book may be reproduced in any form without permission in writing from the publisher, except by a reviewer.

Manufactured in the United States of America

CPSIA compliance information: Batch #CW25ENS: For further information contact Enslow Publishing LLC at 1-800-398-2504.

Please visit our website, www.enslowpublishing.com. For a free color catalog of all our high-quality books, call toll free 1-800-398-2504 or fax 1-877-980-4454.

Find us on

PHOTO CREDITS All images are courtesy of Shutterstock.com, unless otherwise specified. With thanks to Getty Images, Thinkstock Photo and iStockphoto.
Recurring – Tartila, mexrix. Cover – Lauren Suryanata, Subin Kodiyeri, Agarianna76, IgorMass, Nadya_Art, natchapohn. 2–3 – Jacquelyn Johnson. 4–5 – geogif, Ilyshev Dmitry. 6–7 – hagit berkovich, Ljudmila Gluzdovskaja. 8–9 – kristiillustra, Sean R. Stubben, vagabond54. 10–11 – BlueRingMedia, IgorMass, Nazzu. 12–13 – A7880S, MuhammadAliRajput, pzAxe. 14–15 – Wright Out There, Nadya_Art. 16–17 – Krotovych Oleh, Sheril Kannoth, StockSmartStart. 18–19 – Chantelle Bosch, Dmitry Abezgauz, natchapohn. 20–21 – J Curtis, MarySan, Sangaladoola. 22–23 – Abdelrahman Hassanein, Gchapel.

CONTENTS

PAGE 4 Where Am I?
PAGE 6 Fennec Fox
PAGE 8 Gambel's Quail
PAGE 10 Meerkat
PAGE 12 Indian Desert Jird
PAGE 14 Sand Goanna
PAGE 16 Horned Viper
PAGE 18 Camel Spider
PAGE 20 Black-Tailed Jackrabbit
PAGE 22 Hiding in the Habitat
PAGE 24 Glossary and Index

Words that look like this can be found in the glossary on page 24.

WHERE AM I?

Deserts can be very tough <u>environments</u> to live in. Deserts are places where there is very little rain. This means there is not much water for the plants and animals that live there.

Many animals get all the water they need from their food. Some desert animals are <u>predators</u> that sneak up on other animals. Some animals find ways to hide from the animals trying to hunt them.

Habitats give animals everything they need to survive, including food, water, and shelter.

FENNEC FOX

I am a fennec fox. I can be found in sandy deserts such as the Sahara in North Africa. I have a thick fur coat. This keeps me warm when the desert gets very cold during the night.

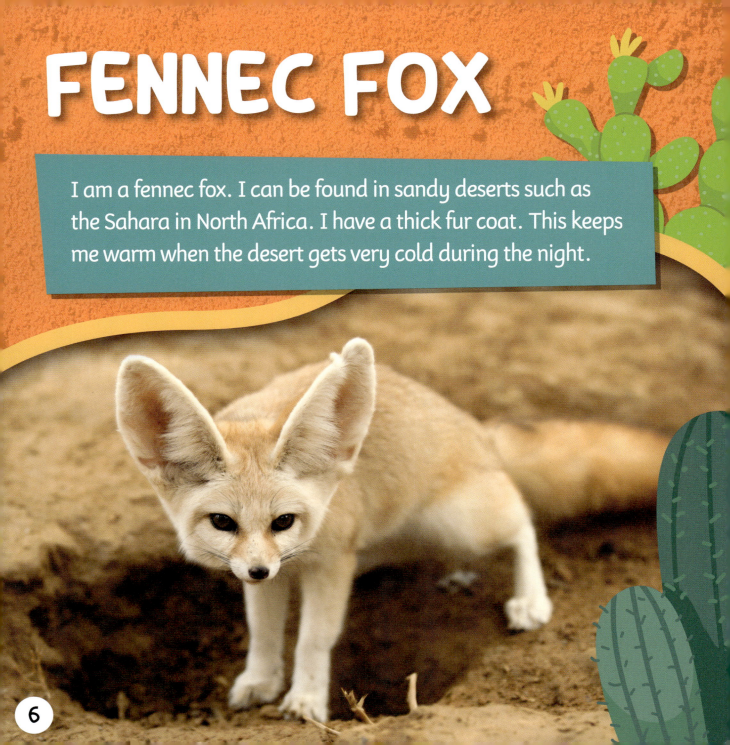

My fur is a sandy color. This helps me <u>camouflage</u> myself by blending in with the sand around me. Camouflage helps me hide from danger. It also helps me sneak up on my <u>prey</u>.

GAMBEL'S QUAIL

I am a Gambel's quail. You can find me in the deserts of Mexico and the United States where some plants grow. I make my nest in the shrubs and trees that can survive in the desert environment.

Can you see me?

Most of my feathers are a dull, gray color. This helps me camouflage with the darker desert plants. I hide in the shade and stay very still to hide from predators.

MEERKAT

Can you find me?

I am a meerkat. I live with my family in the deserts of southern Africa. If you spot one of us, you are very likely to see more meerkats nearby. We can often be seen standing up and looking out across the desert.

We live in underground tunnels called burrows. If one of us spots something dangerous nearby, we make a sound to warn the rest. Then, we all scurry away and hide in our burrows.

INDIAN DESERT JIRD

I am an Indian desert jird. I am a small <u>mammal</u> that can be found in the deserts of India and Pakistan. There are lots of desert predators that try to hunt me.

Can you see me?

I have a clever way of hiding from predators. I dig burrows that have more than one way out. That way, if a predator comes through one hole, I can escape through another!

SAND GOANNA

I am a sand goanna. I am a large lizard. I mostly live in Australia. There are many kinds of goannas. Sand goannas like me often live in deserts. We have much lighter-colored skin compared to other goannas.

HORNED VIPER

I am a horned viper. I am a type of snake that can be found in North Africa and the Middle East. I am a predator. I eat small animals such as birds and lizards.

Can you see my horns?

CAMEL SPIDER

I am a camel spider. I can be found in deserts all around the world. I do not have a skeleton inside my body. Instead, I have something called an exoskeleton on the outside of my body.

I have hairs all over my exoskeleton. They protect me from the heat. My body is a sandy brown color. This helps me to camouflage and hide from predators.

Can you see my hairs?

BLACK-TAILED JACKRABBIT

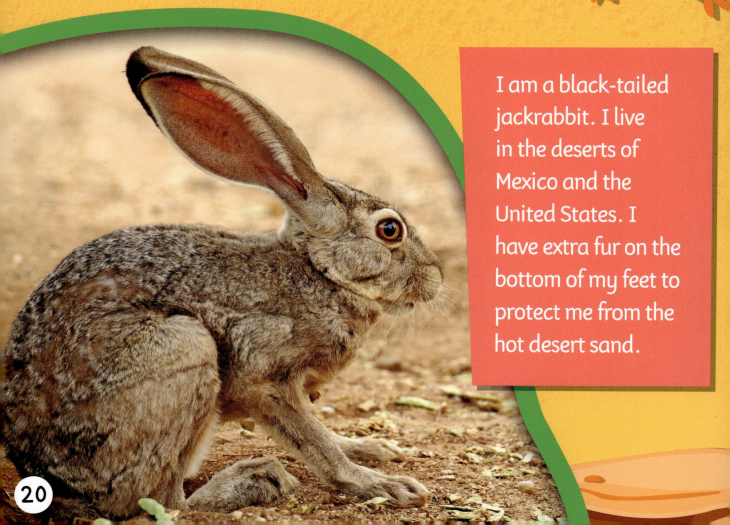

I am a black-tailed jackrabbit. I live in the deserts of Mexico and the United States. I have extra fur on the bottom of my feet to protect me from the hot desert sand.

HIDING IN THE HABITAT

For many animals, staying hidden is an important part of survival. Camouflage helps many animals hide from their predators. For some predators, staying hidden can help them hunt their prey.

A SAGE HEN HIDING IN THE DESERT BRUSH

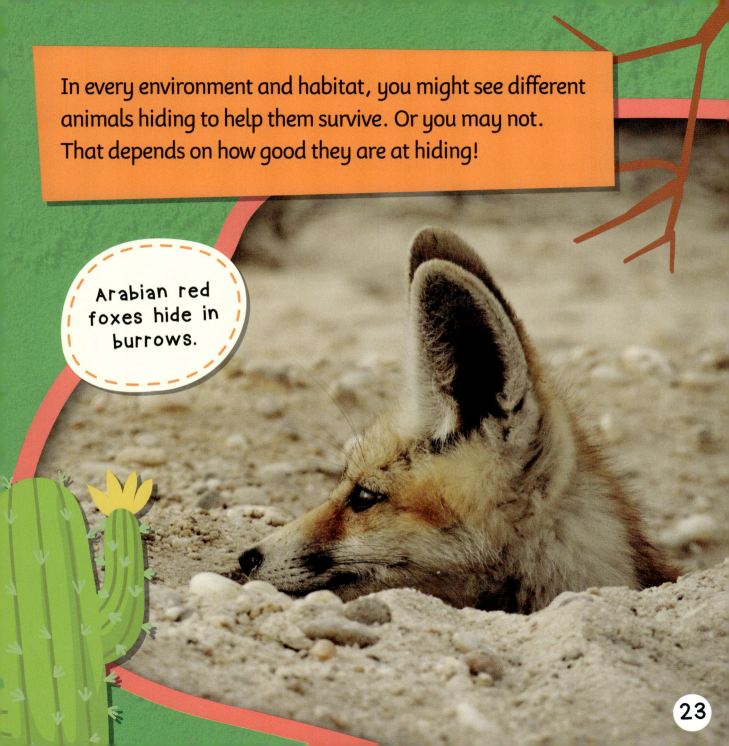

In every environment and habitat, you might see different animals hiding to help them survive. Or you may not. That depends on how good they are at hiding!

Arabian red foxes hide in burrows.

GLOSSARY

CAMOUFLAGE	to blend in with the surroundings
ENVIRONMENTS	the different parts of the natural world
MAMMAL	an animal that is warm-blooded, has a backbone, and produces milk to feed its young
PREDATORS	animals that hunt other animals for food
PREY	animals that are hunted by other animals for food

INDEX

BURROWS 11, 13, 23
FEATHERS 9
FUR 6–7, 20–21
HAIR 19
HORNS 16

SCALES 17
SKIN 14–15
TREES 8
WATER 4–5